VENTURE
MATHEMATICS
WORKSHEETS

Blackline masters for higher ability classes aged 11-16

A. Algebra and Arithmetic

Dr Christian Puritz

TarquinGroup
www.tarquingroup.com

© Tarquin and the Author 2005

ISBN 978 1 89961 870 5

Tarquin,
Suie 74, 17 Holywell Hill
St Albans,
AL1 1DT,
United Kingdom

www.tarquingroup.com

Distributed in the USA by IPG Books
www.ipgbook.com
Printed in the USA by IPG and Partners

A catalogue record for this book is available from the British Library.

Typsetting by Jane Adams
Cover illustration by George Noble

Preface

I wrote most of these worksheets while teaching at an English grammar (i.e. selective) school. Each sheet was motivated by a need felt at the time, to address inadequacies in text book exercises, to deal with new syllabus topics, or simply to follow out some idea. (Two or three have been written more recently for this collection.) They do not comprehensively cover any syllabus, but are provided as a resource to supplement textbooks and other available materials.

The sheets were written for class use in a selective school, so many of them include some fairly routine work, but most also have some hard questions to provide a challenge for the really able, who can get very frustrated when all the work they are given is easy. I have tried to provide guidance in the answer section to help with the hardest questions.

The sheets are classified into four sections: A for algebra and arithmetic, G for geometry, S for statistics, X for extra investigations. The biggest section is G: it just happened that way! (For the 16–18 age range I wrote a lot of statistics sheets, which I hope, God willing, to put together, with some notes on teaching the subject, in due course.)

Sheet G9 on Calculating π has appeared previously in *Mathematics in School*.

I am grateful to my publisher Andrew Griffin for giving much encouragement that spurred me on to do the considerable work involved in preparing the sheets for publication; and also to Jane Adams, the designer, who collaborated with great patience and efficiency in the layout of the final versions of the sheets.

Special thanks are due to my friend George Noble, who used his artistic gifts to produce far better diagrams than I could, as well as helping with the typing. He also, following an idea suggested by Mark Robins, produced the very politically incorrect cover design!

Last but not least, thanks to my wife Cynthia for her longsuffering during all this work, and for help with the checking. Any remaining errors are of course my responsibility. If you discover some and email me, cwpuritz@pmbx.net, I will be grateful, and will respond by sending you details of any other errors that have been found.

I hope you and your pupils will enjoy the venture!

Christian Puritz
January 2006

Contents

Other VMW's are available for:

- Geometry
- Statistics and Xtra Investigations.

© tarquin publications

Thinking decimals

No calculation needed: just *thinking*!

1   Find the values of *a*, *b*, *c* etc. below, giving answers as whole numbers or decimals.

$0.042 = 42 \div a = 42 \times b.$ $9.23 = 923 \div g = 923 \times h.$

$170 = 0.17 \times c = 1.7 \div d.$ $0.09 = 900 \div i = 9 \times j.$

$0.0037 = 3.7 \times e = 3.7 \div f.$

2   Find *a*, *b*, *c* etc.

$17.8 \times 3.09 = 178 \times a.$ $0.132 + 13.08 = (13.2 + 1308) \div f.$

$14.8 \div 5.1 = 148 \div b.$ $5.8 \times 17.2 = 580 \times g.$

$0.096 \times 3500 = 96 \times c.$ $5.8 \div 17.2 = h \div 172.$

$1.39 \times 0.042 = 139 \times 42 \div d.$ $16.4 \div 0.007 = i \div 7.$

$0.42 \div 0.003 = (42 \div 3) \times e.$ $16.4 \times 0.007 = j \times 7.$

In nos. 3 to 7 you are given the answer to a sum, and you write down *without any working* the answers to the sums that follow.

3 $53 \times 72 = 3816.$

(a) 5.3×72 (d) 0.053×7200

(b) 5.3×7.2 (e) $0.0053 \times 72\ 000\ 000$

(c) 0.53×0.72

4 $64 \div 16 = 4$

(a) $640 \div 16$ (d) $0.64 \div 16$

(b) $64 \div 160$ (e) $64 \div 0.16$

(c) $64 \div 1600$ (f) $6.4 \div 0.16$

5 $17.8 \times 14.2 \approx 253.$ (This is not exact, hence the $\approx$ sign. Use the answer as given.)

(a) 17.8×1420 (d) 0.178×0.142

(b) 0.178×14.2 (e) $0.0178 \times 14\ 200$

(c) 1.78×1.42 (f) 178×142

6 $83.9 \div 4.6 \approx 18.2$

(a) $83.9 \div 460$ (d) $839 \div 460$

(b) $8390 \div 4.6$ (e) $0.839 \div 4.6$

(c) $8.39 \div 0.46$ (f) $0.0839 \div 0.046$

7 $3.82^2 \approx 14.6,\ \dfrac{1}{6.82} \approx 0.147$

(a) 38.2^2 (d) $\dfrac{1}{682}$

(b) 382^2 (e) $\dfrac{1}{0.682}$

(c) 0.382^2 (f) $\dfrac{1}{0.00682}$

Thinking decimals *(continued)*

8 In this question *most* of the sums have a simple answer, e.g. 0.001, 0.1, 1, 100. For any that don't, **write N**.

(a) $\dfrac{4.03}{0.403}$

(b) $\dfrac{0.403}{4.03}$

(c) $\dfrac{719}{7.19}$

(d) $\dfrac{7.19}{719}$

(e) $\dfrac{7080}{0.708}$

(f) $\dfrac{0.708}{7080}$

(g) $\dfrac{30.6}{3.6}$

(h) $\dfrac{5.009}{5009}$

(i) $\dfrac{0.013}{0.000013}$

9 Follow the same instructions as for no 8.

(a) $\dfrac{5 \times 4}{0.5 \times 4}$

(b) $\dfrac{4.72 \times 13.8}{0.472 \times 13.8}$

(c) $\dfrac{78 \times 32}{7.8 \times 3.2}$

(d) $\dfrac{53 \times 17}{5.3 \times 0.017}$

(e) $\dfrac{0.63 \times 0.82}{63 \times 82}$

(f) $\dfrac{72 + 38}{7.2 + 3.8}$

(g) $\dfrac{3.91 + 4.84}{391 + 484}$

(h) $\dfrac{38 + 17}{3.8 + 17}$

(i) $\dfrac{3.4 \times 0.096}{0.034 \times 9.6}$

(j) $\dfrac{0.503^3}{50.3^3}$

10 In each part the answer is fairly close to one of the following numbers:

0.003,   0.02,   0.15,   0.3,   1.5,   8,   15,   20,   30,   80,   150,   200,   300,   800.

Without working out the sum in full, find which number is nearest the answer. E.g. for 3.92×2.01 do 4×2 to give 8.

(a) 4.03×19.9

(b) 0.036×0.08

(c) 16.1×49.7

(d) 0.052×298

(e) 1.05×20.2

(f) $1 \div 0.12$

(g) $3.68 \div 0.018$

(h) $0.152 \div 51$

(i) $4.96 \div 0.248$

(j) $3.08 \div 2.01$

11 This continues no 10, with the same set of numbers as answers.

(a) $3.06 \times 1.98 \div 300$

(b) $0.75 \times 2.1 \div 5$

(c) $\dfrac{4.96 \times 3.02}{0.0098 \times 10.4}$

(d) 0.55^2

(e) $\dfrac{0.000156}{0.000099}$

(f) $0.71^2 - 0.59^2$

(g) $20.2 - 16.2 \times 0.0098$ (do × first!)

(h) $200 - 0.00042 \times 0.036$

(i) $17.8 \times 0.102 + 0.309 \times 19.6$

(j) $\dfrac{398.4 \times 15.2 \times 0.0015}{0.0031 \times 2.48 \times 4.06}$

Patterns and problem solving with algebra

1 If you add up three consecutive integers (whole numbers), e.g. 15, 16 and 17, is the total always a multiple of 3? And if you add up four consecutive integers, is the total a multiple of 4? Let's investigate:

(a) Let the first of three consecutive integers be n. Write down what the other two are, in terms of n, and show that the total is $3n + 3$. What can you conclude?

(b) Now take n to be the first of four consecutive integers. Write down the others, form their total and explain how you can prove from this that the total is always even, but is never a multiple of 4.

(c) Show also that, if you multiply the two outer numbers (1st and 4th) of four consecutive integers, the product is always less than the product of the two inner numbers (2nd and 3rd); by how much is it less?

2 A number that is known to be even can be written as $2n$, with n standing for any integer. Hence a number that is known to be odd can be written as $2n + 1$ or as $2n - 1$.

(a) Using $2n$ to stand for the first number, show that the sum of four consecutive even numbers is always a multiple of 4, but is never a multiple of 8.

(b) Show that the sum of four consecutive odd numbers is always a multiple of 8.

(c) Investigate, as in 1(c), the difference between the product of the two outer numbers and that of the two inner numbers in a set of four consecutive odd numbers.

3 **Twin primes** are prime numbers differing by 2. The first few pairs of twins are 3 and 5, 5 and 7, 11 and 13, 17 and 19. Adding the two primes in each pair gives totals 8, 12, 24 and 36 respectively.

(a) Find the other twin primes below 100, and total each pair. Are the totals still multiples of 12?

There are many, many more twin primes, possibly infinitely many: no-one knows yet for sure. Are their totals still multiples of 12? The next part investigates this question.

(b) Show that the number in between two twin primes must be even, and explain why (except when the twins are 3 and 5) it must be a multiple of 3. Hence this number is a multiple of 6, and we can write it as $6n$, where n stands for an integer. Now express the twin primes themselves, and their total, using n, and hence show that the total is always a multiple of 12, apart from the very first total. Why is that an exception?

4 The **digit sum** of a number is just the sum of the digits; e.g. for 4508 it is 17.

(a) Find the digit sum for the following numbers: 38, 76, 23, 89. Then subtract the digit sum for each number from the number itself, e.g. for 47 you would do $47 - 11 = 36$. Which of the multiplication tables contains all the answers?

(b) Suppose that a two digit number N has tens digit a and units digit b. The number is then $N = 10a + b$, while the digit sum S is just $a + b$. Form the difference $D = N - S$ and hence show that D is always a multiple of 9.

(c) Find N, S and D for a three digit number with digits a, b, c, and show that D is again a multiple of 9; repeat with a six digit number.

(d) Use the results of (b) and (c) to explain why, if the digit sum of a number N is divisible by 3, or by 9, then so is N itself.

(e) Without doing any division, find the remainder when 764 038 is divided by 9.

Patterns and problem solving with algebra
(continued)

5   The number 39 has the property that it is equal to the digit sum 12 plus the digit product 27 (= 3 × 9).

   (a) Taking a two digit number N to have digits a and b, form an equation to express the fact that $N = S + P$, where S and P are the digit sum and product; hence find all two digit numbers with this property.

   (b) Find all two digit numbers N for which $N - S = 3P$, and show that there are none for which $N - S = 2P$.

6   (a) You are required to find a two digit number N which is equal to 4 times its digit sum S. Taking the digits to be a and b, show that the requirements leads to the equation $2a = b$; hence find all such N.

   Find similarly all two digit numbers for which the ratio N/S is

   (b) 2   (c) 5   (d) 7.

7   When the two digit number $N = 12$ is reversed, it gives the number $R = 21$, which is 75% greater than N.

   (a) To find other numbers with this property, let N have digits a, b, and explain why $10b + a = 1.75(10a + b)$. Simplify this equation and hence find all N for which R is 75% greater than N.

   Now find likewise any two digit numbers N such that

   (b) R is 20% greater than N (c) R is $62\frac{1}{2}$% less than N (d) R is 240% greater than N.

8   Can the difference between a number N and the reversed number R ever be a prime number? Investigate this, using algebra, for two digit, three digit and five digit numbers.

9   Algernon found that, on his birthday in 1995, his age was one fifty sixth of the year of his birth. Let his age then be a years. Use the given information to form and solve an equation for a. Bertrand found that his age in 1984 was one thirty first of the year of his birth, while Cyril reckons that, if he lives till 2030, he will then be one twenty eighth of the year of his birth. How old were they in 2000?

10   (a) The average of Peter's and Quentin's ages is 15, that of Quentin's and Raja's is 19, while Raja and Sarah have an average age of 13. What is the average of Peter's and Sarah's ages? (One method is to let Peter's age be p and work out the other ages in terms of p.)

   (b) Repeat (a) with the given averages being a, b and c respectively.

11   It is a familiar fact of algebra that, for all numbers p, q, r, $p \times (q + r) = (p \times q) + (p \times r)$. (This says that multiplication is distributive over addition, and is used, in the simpler form $p(q + r) = pq + pr$, whenever we open brackets.) However, the same statement with + and × interchanged, namely "$p + (q \times r) = (p + q) \times (p + r)$" is not true in general. Can you find out for what sort of values of p, q, r it actually is true?

12   Martin did a mountain walk and came back by the same route, taking 5 hours altogether. His walking speeds were 3mph uphill, 6mph downhill and 4mph on the level. What was the total distance he walked?

   (Let the uphill, downhill and level distances on the outward journey be u, d, l miles respectively, and form an equation. You will not be able to find u, d, l individually, but you can still find the total distance.)

Further problem solving with algebra

13 There was a power cut from 11 till 11.30 pm last night, after which my electric clock, which had been correct at 11, started going backwards at half its usual speed. Curiously, this morning when I turned on the radio and heard the time, the clock was showing the right time! Can you tell me what time that was?

(Let it be *x* hours past midnight. Write down what time the clock then shows, and make an equation.)

14 This problem comes from the famous Swiss mathematician Leonhard Euler:

A man left money in his will for his sons when he died.

The first son was given 100 crowns plus one tenth of the remainder, the second received 200 crowns plus one tenth of the remainder, the third had 300 crowns plus one tenth of the remainder, and so on down to the last.

It turned out that, in spite of these complicated instructions, each son inherited the same amount of money.

How much was the total estate, and how many sons were there?

(Let the total be *T* crowns. Work out carefully what the first and second sons inherit, in terms of *T*, then equate these two, solve for *T*; then check that the story works out for all the sons.)

15 In a small school there are two sets of boys, called A and B, with three boys in each set. The IQs of all the boys are known, and it is found that, when Tom, with IQ 125, transfers from A to B, the average IQ within each set increases by 5. What were the averages before? To answer this, let the average IQ in the A set before transfer be *a*. Write down the total of the IQs in A before the transfer, then the total after the transfer, then the new average IQ in A, and hence show that

$$\frac{3a - 125}{2} = a + 5.$$

Solve this to find the previous average IQ in set A. Similarly, using another equation, find the previous average IQ in set B.

16 A very accurate clock has its minute hand exactly on one of the minute marks, when the hour hand is exactly two minute marks away. At what time does this occur?

(The hour hand moves 5 minute marks per hour, so one every 12 minutes. The event in the question must happen at a multiple of 12 minutes past an hour. Let it be at 12*k* minutes after *h* o'clock. Work out where each hand is then, and make an equation from the fact that the difference must be 2 or –2. At the end use trial to find *h* and *k*.)

17 The number 45, called the *total*, can be divided into four *parts*, namely 8, 12, 5 and 20, that all give the same answer when doing adding, subtracting, multiplying and dividing, using the *operating number* 2; that is, $8 + 2 = 12 - 2 = 5 \times 2 = 20 \div 2$; the *result* of each is 10.

(a) Find the four parts into which the total 50 can be divided, using the operating number 4. (Let *r* be the result; express the parts *a*, *b*, *c*, *d* in terms of *r*, then use the total being 50 to make an equation.)

(b) Given the total 98, can you find the four parts and an operating number? (Call the result *r* and the operating number *n*, write an equation again; you will need some trial to find a solution with *n* and *r* being whole numbers.)

(c) Repeat (b) with total 99, and show that it can't be done (using integers) with total 95.

(d) Investigate further to find for what total numbers the division into four parts can be done, and how to find the operating number and the parts.

Equations

Solve these equations; give answers in decimal form for those which contain decimals, otherwise as fractions or mixed numbers. Most come out exactly by *cancelling*. For the few that don't, give answers correct to 3 significant figures.

1 $3\frac{1}{2}x = 2\frac{1}{3}$

2 $3\frac{1}{4}b = 8\frac{1}{8}$

3 $\frac{2}{3}y = \frac{7}{9}$

4 $0.8u = 1.28$

5 $0.5v = 6.3$

6 $\frac{4}{9}y = 1\frac{7}{9}$

7 $0.36a = 14.4$

8 $3\frac{1}{2}c = 17\frac{1}{2}$

9 $0.75a = 60$

10 $0.03p = 0.63$

11 $0.042x = 2.1$

12 $3.9y = 0.065$

13 $4.6u = 0.345$

14 $0.6a = 38.2$

15 $2.8y = 0.056$

16 $\frac{x}{5} = 7$

17 $\frac{y}{8} = 4$

18 $\frac{x}{3.6} = 0.04$

19 $\frac{a}{0.03} = 0.28$

20 $\frac{4x}{17} = \frac{11}{68}$

21 $\frac{3x}{4} = 2$

22 $\frac{5x}{6} = \frac{2}{3}$

23 $\frac{a}{1.8} = 0.02$

24 $\frac{b}{0.045} = 20$

25 $\frac{0.7u}{4.8} = 3.5$

26 $\frac{1.2u}{0.39} = \frac{0.24}{0.65}$

27 $\frac{0.48x}{1.95} = \frac{1.44}{6.5}$

28 $\frac{3000a}{0.55} = 60$

29 $\frac{100c}{0.96} = \frac{1}{12}$

30 $\frac{0.002p}{0.56} = \frac{4}{7}$

31 $1.5a = 0.33$

32 $\frac{6b}{7} = 5\frac{1}{3}$

33 $0.18u = 0.009$

34 $\frac{v}{0.002} = 3000$

35 $\frac{5a}{7.2} = 4.5$

36 $\frac{3y}{0.014} = 2100$

37 $150a = 0.03$

38 $0.15u = 3.8$

39 $\frac{0.04c}{3000} = 0.008$

40 $\frac{450x}{0.064} = \frac{0.27}{128}$

41 $\frac{1}{a} = 4$

42 $\frac{1}{x} = 0.05$

43 $\frac{10.5}{a} = 3$

44 $\frac{7}{b} = 2$

45 $\frac{4}{x} = 24$

46 $\frac{6}{a} = 0.4$

47 $\frac{0.05}{w} = 1.2$

48 $\frac{1.35}{p} = 0.27$

49 $\frac{0.12}{r} = 1.6$

50 $\frac{2000}{u} = 0.16$

51 $\frac{3}{5x} = \frac{4}{7}$

52 $\frac{5}{2y} = 100$

53 $\frac{0.8}{3y} = \frac{0.01}{6}$

54 $\frac{13}{0.06u} = \frac{0.65}{0.018}$

55 $\frac{0.04}{p} = 250$

56 $0.19y = 380$

57 $\frac{x}{0.84} = 0.02$

58 $\frac{3.5u}{5.7} = \frac{0.49}{0.019}$

59 $\frac{0.01}{v} = 50$

60 $\frac{3.84}{0.07x} = \frac{0.144}{0.035}$

Cancelling

Calculate the following, cancelling whenever possible: in some cases you must factorise first. Leave answers, if they aren't whole numbers, as decimals (exact, or correct to 3 sig. figs.) if there are decimals in the sum, otherwise as fractions or mixed numbers.

1 $\dfrac{56 \times 38}{19 \times 140}$

2 $\dfrac{48 \times 484}{176 \times 72}$

3 $\dfrac{3.96 \times 0.6}{1.2 \times 0.33}$

4 $\dfrac{0.88 \times 3.5}{5.6 \times 0.11}$

5 $\dfrac{0.6 \times 3.2}{1.2 \times 0.64}$

6 $\dfrac{200 \times 0.39}{650 \times 0.6}$

7 $\dfrac{55 \times 0.34}{5.1 \times 2.2}$

8 $\dfrac{0.08 \times 330}{0.88 \times 300}$

9 $\dfrac{0.049 \times 7.2}{0.063}$

10 $\dfrac{1.44}{3.2 \times 0.18}$

11 $\dfrac{1.92 \times 0.315}{3.36 \times 0.15}$

12 $\dfrac{0.416 \times 0.91}{1.69 \times 32}$

13 $\dfrac{5800 \times 0.42}{5.6 \times 87}$

14 $\dfrac{5200 \times 0.08}{64 \times 1.3}$

15 $\dfrac{540}{2.88 \times 1.5}$

16 $\dfrac{1.6 \times 3.8}{0.19 \times 0.4}$

17 $\dfrac{0.65 \times 0.64}{1.2 \times 1.3}$

18 $\dfrac{0.036 \times 400}{240 \times 1.5}$

19 $\dfrac{0.625 \times 1.43}{3.25 \times 0.44}$

20 $\dfrac{6300 \times 0.77}{880 \times 4.9}$

21 $\dfrac{4}{9} \times 16 + \dfrac{4}{9} \times 20$

22 $\dfrac{3}{7} \times 50 + \dfrac{3}{7} \times 6$

23 $\dfrac{7}{16} \times 13 + \dfrac{7}{16} \times 35$

24 $\dfrac{3}{8} \times 0.41 + \dfrac{3}{8} \times 0.03$

25 $\dfrac{22}{7} \times 5.94 - \dfrac{22}{7} \times 0.34$

26 $3\frac{1}{2} \times 0.59 - 3\frac{1}{2} \times 0.57$

27 $0.42 \times 13.5 + 0.42 \times 6.5$

28 $0.96 \times 13.7 - 0.96 \times 12.2$

29 $\dfrac{22}{7} \times 4.86 + \dfrac{22}{7} \times 9.14$

30 $6\frac{2}{9} \times \frac{5}{7} + 3\frac{1}{9} \times 1\frac{1}{7}$

31 $0.62 \times 7.5 + 0.31 \times 5$

32 $1.48 \times 2.7 + 0.74 \times 4.6$

33 $3.6 \times 4.1 + 2.4 \times 1.35$

34 $35 \times 0.736 - 28 \times 0.170$

35 $\dfrac{22}{7} \times 0.44 + \dfrac{44}{7} \times 0.48$

36 $\dfrac{32 \times 8 + 32 \times 6}{16 \times 28}$

37 $\dfrac{15 \times 48}{24 \times 53 + 24 \times 7}$

38 $\dfrac{16 \times 9 + 16 \times 12}{63 \times 25 + 63 \times 7}$

39 $\dfrac{7.5 \times 0.03 + 7.5 \times 0.13}{0.08 \times 0.15}$

40 $\dfrac{0.92 \times 3.8 + 10.08 \times 3.8}{2.2 \times 1.45 + 2.2 \times 0.45}$

41 $\dfrac{0.06 \times 1.35 + 0.06 \times 1.45}{0.34 \times 120 + 3.86 \times 120}$

42 $\dfrac{0.13 \times 3.8 + 0.26 \times 4.1}{0.36 \times 0.17 + 0.84 \times 0.02}$

43 $\dfrac{350 \times 0.6 - 490 \times 0.09}{1.58 \times 6.32 - 1.58 \times 2.12}$

44 $\dfrac{22}{7} \times (0.43)^2 - \dfrac{22}{7} \times (0.27)^2$

45 $\dfrac{4}{9} \times 34.8^2 - \dfrac{4}{9} \times 1.2^2$

46 $\dfrac{22}{7} \times 61.3^2 - \dfrac{22}{7} \times 8.7^2$

47 $\dfrac{1.3}{4.8} \times \dfrac{0.18^2 - 0.06^2}{0.78}$

48 $\dfrac{0.89 \times 8.2}{17.1^2 - 0.7^2}$

49 $\dfrac{3.62^2 - 1.38^2}{7.5^2 - 0.5^2}$

50 $(4.42^2 - 3.58^2) \times \dfrac{22}{7 \times 1.32}$

51 $\dfrac{0.34 \times 0.063}{0.09 \times 5.1}$

52 $\dfrac{22}{7} \times 3.92 - \dfrac{22}{7} \times 2.94$

53 $0.317 \times 6.381 + 0.317 \times 3.619$

54 $\dfrac{44}{7} \times 13.2 - \dfrac{22}{7} \times 22.9$

55 $\dfrac{3}{16} \times 0.73^2 - \dfrac{3}{16} \times 0.07^2$

56 $\dfrac{\frac{3}{14} \times 0.68}{\frac{5}{7} \times 0.51}$

57 $\dfrac{6.34^2 - 1.66^2}{1.3 \times 16}$

58 $\dfrac{192.6^2 - 107.4^2}{57.6^2 - 27.6^2}$

59 $\dfrac{0.049 \times 0.51}{1.7 \times 0.21}$

60 $(5.63^2 - 1.37^2) \times \dfrac{0.3}{7}$

Indices and standard form

1 Given $a = 10^{-2}$, $b = 10^6$, $c = 10^3$, find without using a calculator,

(1) ab (2) $\dfrac{b}{a}$ (3) a^2c (4) $\dfrac{c^3}{b}$ (5) $\sqrt{\dfrac{a}{b}}$

(6) $\sqrt[3]{bc}$ (7) $(abc)^{-2}$ (8) $(bc^2)^{\frac{1}{4}}$ (9) $\dfrac{(3a)^2}{3a^2}$ (10) $\dfrac{(bc)^3}{bc^3}$

2 Redo no.1 with $a = 10^4$, $b = 10^{-6}$, $c = 10^{-3}$.

3 You are given the following approximations to certain physical constants: $N = 6 \times 10^{23}$, $c = 3 \times 10^8$, $m = 9 \times 10^{-31}$, $e = 1.6 \times 10^{-19}$ and $h = 10^{-34}$. Find in standard form, without calculator:

(1) $\dfrac{N}{c}$ (2) $\dfrac{1}{h}$ (3) $\dfrac{c^2}{m}$ (4) mc^2 (5) $\sqrt{e}$

(6) Ne (7) c^3 (8) mh^{-1} (9) $\dfrac{ec^2}{N}$ (10) $m + 100h$

4 The sun is about 150 million km from the earth, and light travels at 300 000 km/s.

(a) Express these data in standard form.

(b) How long does it take, in minutes and seconds, for light to reach earth from the sun?

(c) How long would it take if light only travelled at 70mph? (1mile = 1.6km.)

5 (a) A light-year is the distance light travels in a year. Express this in km and in miles, in standard form, to 3SF. (Take 1 year as $365\frac{1}{4}$ days, to allow for leap years.)

(b) The nearest star, Proxima Centauri, is about $4\frac{1}{4}$ light years away. A space shuttle, travelling at its usual orbiting speed, would take 100 000 years to reach this star. Find the shuttle's speed in km/s and in mph.

6 The masses of a proton and an electron are 1.673×10^{-27} and 9.110×10^{-31} kg.

(a) How many electrons have the same mass as one proton?

(b) How many protons would have a total mass of 1kg?

7 A display in the Science Museum informs us that if the atoms in your hand were scaled up to the size of peas, then your hand would be big enough to hold the earth. Taking the earth as having diameter 12800 km, a pea's diameter as 4mm and a sphere that you can hold as having diameter 8cm, calculate an estimate of the diameter of an atom, giving your answer in mm in standard form to 2SF.

8 Solve

(a) $x^{-3} = 27$ (b) $x^{\frac{1}{2}} = 0.1$ (c) $x^{\frac{2}{3}} = 16$ (d) $x^{-\frac{1}{4}} = 10$.

9 A sum of £1000 is invested in a savings account and 6% is added to the account at the end of each year; the interest is said to be *compounded annually* because the interest for the first year helps to earn more interest in the second year, and so on.

(a) By what factor is the amount in the account multiplied each year?

(b) What is the amount after n years? Evaluate this for $n = 10$.

(c) What rate of interest would be needed to double the amount in 10 years?

(d) What rate would give 50% growth in 5 years?

Reading and drawing graphs

1 Figure 1 shows the height at various times of a stone catapulted up from ground level.

   (a) How long is the stone in the air?

   (b) What is its greatest height, and when is this reached?

   (c) Find its height after

       (1) 4 s

       (2) 1.3 s

       (3) 0.7 s.

   (d) Find when its height is

       (1) 25 m

       (2) 10 m.

   (e) For how long is the stone over 35m above the ground?

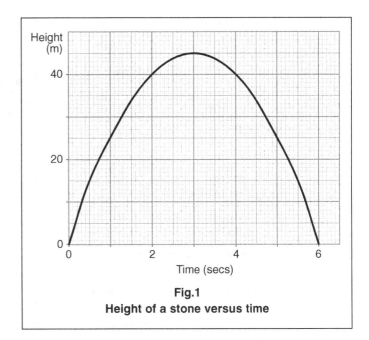

Fig.1
Height of a stone versus time

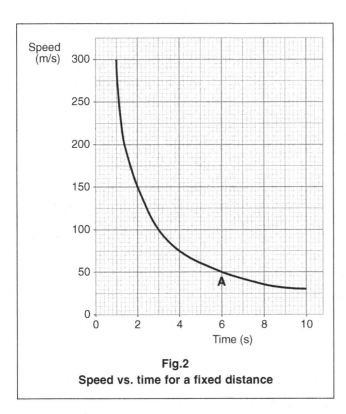

Fig.2
Speed vs. time for a fixed distance

2 Figure 2 shows the speeds needed by a car to cover a certain fixed distance in various times.

   (a) What speed is needed to cover the distance in

       (1) 3.4 s

       (2) 7.3 s?

   (b) How long does the journey take at

       (1) 225 m/s

       (2) 62 m/s?

   (c) Use the coordinates of the point A to calculate how great the fixed distance is.

Reading and drawing graphs *(continued)*

3 Figure 3 shows the volume V (continuous curve) and surface area A (dotted curve) of a sphere, plotted against the radius r. Units are not specified and need not be given, except in part (c).

(a) Find V and A for

   (1) $r = 2.35$ (2) $r = 3.8$.

(b) Find r when

   (1) $V = 620$ (2) $A = 400$

(c) Find, giving units,

   (1) the volume of a sphere of surface area 250 cm^2

   (2) the area of a sphere of volume 900 km^3.

(d) For what value of r does $V = A$? What would be the volume and surface area of a cube just big enough to contain a sphere with this radius?

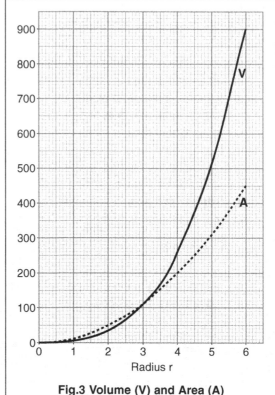

Fig.3 Volume (V) and Area (A) of a sphere versus radius (r)

4 The Highway Code gives the following information about the distances an average car needs in normal road conditions to come to rest from various speeds:

Speed of car in mph	30	50	70
Thinking distance (before brakes are applied) in feet	30	50	70
Braking distance in feet	45	125	245
Total stopping distance in feet	75	175	315

(a) Try to work out what formula is being used to give the braking distances, and hence extend the table so as to deal with speeds from 0 to 80 mph in steps of 10 mph. Draw on one diagram, in different colours, graphs of thinking, braking and total distance (vertically) against speed (horizontally). Use graph paper in portrait position, with scales 2 cm to 10 mph and 2 cm to 50 ft.

(b) Give your diagram a brief title, label the three graphs clearly and write a paragraph on the same page explaining more fully what they are about.

(c) Find the total distance when the speed is

   (1) 35 mph   (2) 52 mph.

Check your answers by calculation.

(d) For what speeds is

   (1) the braking distance more than the thinking distance,

   (2) the total distance less than 100 yards (300 ft),

   (3) the total distance 100 ft more than the thinking distance?

(e) Given that there are 1760 yards to a mile and 3600 seconds to an hour, work out how much time the Highway Code is allowing for thinking before the brakes are applied.

Reading and drawing graphs (Extension questions)

5 When a stone is thrown up from ground level at a speed of v m/s (metres per second) the height h metres after t seconds is given approximately by the formula $h = vt - 5t^2$.

(a) Copy and complete the following table to give values of $5t^2$ for values of t from 0 to 8 in steps of 0.5.

t	0	0.5	1	1.5	2	2.5 etc.
t^2	0	0.25	1	2.25		
$5t^2$	0	1.25	5	11.25 etc		

(b) For a stone thrown at speed $v = 10$ m/s, $h = 10t - 5t^2$. Copy the following table and continue it until you get $h = 0$, i.e. until the stone reaches the ground.

t	0	0.5	1 etc.
$10t$	0	5	10
$-5t^2$	0	−1.25	−5
$10t - 5t^2$	0	3.75	5

(c) Repeat (b) for stones thrown up at 20, 30 and 40 m/s.

(d) Draw on one diagram graphs of height (on the vertical axis) against time (horizontal axis) for the four speeds. Use portrait position with scales 2 cm to 1 s, 2 cm to 10 m. Title the diagram and label the four graphs clearly.

(e) Make a table showing the total time of flight T and the greatest height reached, H, for each speed v. Suggest formulae for T and H in terms of v, and use them to predict

    (1) T and H when $v = 35$,

    (2) what speed is needed to throw a stone 245 m up.

6 Sums and products

Put the origin near the bottom left corner of your graph paper, and use scales 2 cm to 10 units for x and y. Draw on this one page all the following, for positive coordinates only, using one colour for those in (a) and another for (b).

(a) Graphs of $x + y = s$, with $s = 20$, then $s = 40$, then 60, then 80, then 100.

(b) Graphs of $xy = p$, with $p = 100$, then $p = 400$, then 900, then 1600, then 2500.

For these you can take $x = 1, 1.5, 2, 2.5, 3, 4, 5, 6, 8, 10, 12.5, 15, 20, 25, 30, 40, 50, 60$ and 80 and find y for each x. Ignore any points that are off the page.

Use your graphs to answer the following:

(c) Find x and y given $x + y = 60$, $xy = 400$.

(d) Find the dimensions of a rectangle with area 900 m^2 and perimeter 160 m.

(e) If you know that $x + y = 40$, what is the maximum possible value of xy?

(f) If a rectangle has area 100 cm^2, what is the minimum perimeter it can have?

Straight line graphs applied

General notes: Always **title** your diagrams so a reader knows what they are about. If there are several graphs on one diagram, **label** each clearly. Always draw the axes along the thicker lines on the paper, not half-way in between them. Use simple scales; it is not necessary to use up all the graph paper. Scale numbers on the axes should be written every 2cm.

1   **Cooking times for chicken**

Sometimes the instructions specify 25 minutes per pound weight, sometimes they say 20 minutes per pound plus 20 minutes. (Nowadays the instructions refer to "per 500 g" rather than "per pound," although 1 lb (i.e 1 pound) is 454 g. To keep things simple we'll stick to pounds.) We'll call these methods A and B respectively. If the weight of a chicken is x lb then the cooking time in minutes is either $y_A = 25x$ or $y_B = 20x + 20$.

(a) Make a table showing values of y_A and y_B for $x = 0, 2, 4, 6$.

(b) Draw on one diagram graphs of y_A and y_B against x, for x from 0 to 6. Scales are 2cm to 1 unit for x, 2cm to 20 minutes for y. Use your graphs to find:

(c) y_A and y_B when $x = 2.5$,

(d) the weight of a chicken that takes two hours and ten minutes to cook by method B,

(e) for what values of x the times differ by not more than 5 minutes,

(f) which of y_A, y_B is directly proportional to x.

2   **Revs per minute**

My car has a revolution counter to show how fast the engine is turning. When the speed is 10mph, the counter shows either 1200 or 2000 revs/min. At 20mph it shows 1600, 2400 or 4000 revs/min, at 40mph it reads 1800, 2200 or 3200, and at 60mph the engine speed is 2700 or 3300 revs/min.

Plot points for these data, taking car speed in mph on the x axis and engine speed on the y axis. Use 2cm to 10mph and 2cm to 1000revs/min.

(a) The graph of engine speed against car speed should be a straight line through the origin. Why? Join the points you have plotted to the origin. How many straight lines do you have to draw? Why are there several lines?

(b) Find the gradient and write down the equation of each line.

(c) How many revs/min could the engine be doing at 30mph?

(d) What is the least engine speed when cruising at 70mph?

(e) The engine is liable to stall at below 1000 revs/min, and gets excessively noisy above 4000 revs/min. What range of speeds is available in each gear?

(f) If the engine does n revolutions in travelling 1 mile in 1st gear, how many does it do in 1 mile in each of the other gears, in terms of n? Can you find n?

Straight line graphs applied *(continued)*

3 Celsius to Fahrenheit

When Fahrenheit devised his temperature scale, he made 0° be the lowest temperature he could produce, (with a mixture of salt and ice) and 100° to be human body temperature (though this is now taken to be 98.4°F). The Celsius (or Centigrade) scale makes 0 and 100 to be the freezing point and boiling point of water; and these were found to be 32 and 212 respectively on the Fahrenheit scale. Thus on a graph for converting Celsius to Fahrenheit two points are (0, 32) and (100, 212).

(a) Find the gradient of this graph, and its equation, in the form $F = aC + b$.

Plot the graph, taking C from −100 to 300, with 2cm per 50°C and 2 cm per 100°F. Use it to convert

(b) −50°, 80° and 190° C to °F, and

(c) 0°, 70° and 425°F to °C.

(d) Find x if $x°C = x°F$, using the graph, and also by algebra.

4 Approximate conversions

This question continues from no. 3. Two approximate conversion formulae are $F_1 = 2C + 30$ and $F_2 = 2C$. Plot these on the same diagram you have made for no. 3.

(a) For which values of C are these formulae exactly right? Answer from the graphs and by algebra.

(b) For which ranges of values of C are the errors in using F_1 and F_2 less than 10°F? Give separate answers for F_1 and F_2, again using graphs and then algebra.

(c) For what range is F_1 less than 1°F wrong?

(d) One of the approximate formulae is used for air temperatures in weather predictions, and one is for oven temperatures.

Identify which formula is the appropriate one for each purpose.

(e) For what values does the oven temperature conversion formula produce an answer that is different from the correct answer by 1% or less of the correct answer?

Number patterns and algebra

1   (a)   Take two consecutive integers, say 7 and 8. Find the difference between their squares: $8^2 - 7^2 = 15$.
         What do you notice about 7, 8 and 15? Try some more pairs of consecutive integers.

    (b)   Make a statement about the difference between the squares of any two consecutive integers,
         and prove your statement algebraically.

2   (a)   Calculate the squares of $1\frac{1}{2}$, $2\frac{1}{2}$, $3\frac{1}{2}$, $4\frac{1}{2}$, $5\frac{1}{2}$, as mixed numbers.

    (b)   State a rule for finding the square of an integer plus a half, and prove your rule algebraically.

    Use your rule to find without calculator

    (c) $(20\frac{1}{2})^2$ (d) $(100.5)^2$ (e) 65^2.

3   (a)   Take three consecutive integers, say 7, 8 and 9. Square them and find the average of the
         squares, $\dfrac{7^2 + 8^2 + 9^2}{3}$, expressed as a mixed number.

         How does it differ from 8^2?

    (b)   Repeat with some other sets of three consecutive numbers, and find a quick way of predicting
         what the answer will be.

    (c)   What will the average of $(n - 1)^2$, n^2 and $(n + 1)^2$ be? Prove your answer.

    (d)   Write down the values of

         (i) $\dfrac{99^2 + 100^2 + 101^2}{3}$ (ii) $499^2 + 500^2 + 501^2$.

    (e)   Investigate numerically and by algebra the average of the squares of five consecutive integers.
         Try other numbers of integers if you like! (The difference between the mean of the squares and
         the square of the mean of any set of numbers is called the variance of the set; it is the square
         of the standard deviation, used in statistics as a measure of spread. There is a formula for the
         variance of any set of k consecutive integers in terms of k, which you can try to find, if you are
         feeling enterprising!)

4   Calculate the value of $n^3 - n$ for $n = 2, 3, 4, 5, 6$. What is the highest common factor of all the
    answers? Would you get the same HCF if you continued taking further values of n, however far you
    went? Justify your answer by considering the factors of $n^3 - n$.

5   Find the remainders when 3^2, 5^2, 7^2, 9^2 and 11^2 are divided by 8. What do you infer? Can you prove
    algebraically that your inference is always correct?

6   Can the squares of two integers differ by (a) 15 (b) 30 (c) 60? Prove your answers. For what values
    of k can the difference between two squares be equal to k?

7   (a)   Multiply together 3, 4, 5 and 6; add 1 to the answer, then take the square root. Try this with
         other sets of four consecutive integers. What do you notice?

    (b)   If the integers are n, $n + 1$, $n + 2$ and $n + 3$, what would you expect the answer to be? Try to
         prove this algebraically.

    (c)   Write down without using a calculator the square root of $97 \times 98 \times 99 \times 100 + 1$.

8   (a)   Calculate $\sqrt{5^2 + 6^2 + 30^2}$, $\sqrt{8^2 + 9^2 + 72^2}$ and $\sqrt{20^2 + 21^2 + 420^2}$.

    (b)   Can you guess the values of $\sqrt{10^2 + 11^2 + 110^2}$ and $\sqrt{30^2 + 31^2 + 930^2}$?

    (c)   Investigate algebraically whether the pattern always works.

The effect of errors on calculations

1   Given that $x = 3.50$ and $y = 2.78$, each correct to 3SF, find greatest and least values for

   (a) x

   (b) $x + y$

   (c) $x - y$

   (d) $\dfrac{1}{y}$

   [Answers (a) 3.505, 3.495 (b) 6.29, 6.27 (c) 0.73, 0.71 (d) 0.36036, 0.35907. Check that you agree!]

2   (a) Find exactly the least and greatest values of $a(b + c)$ and $a \div (b - c)$ if $a = 3.2$, $b = 5.1$, $c = 4.9$, correct to 2SF.

   (b) Repeat (a) taking values of a, b and c to be 3.20, 5.10, 4.90, correct to 3SF; give all answers to 5SF.

3   (a) Calculate the volume of a sphere of radius 10.0cm, using the formula $\frac{4}{3}\pi r^3$. Store the answer in memory.

   (b) If the radius is correct to 1DP, find the least and greatest values of the volume, and express the difference between them as a percentage of the answer in (a), to 3SF.

   (c) Repeat (a) and (b) using surface area, given by $4\pi r^2$, instead of volume.

4   (a) Andrew measured the angle of elevation of the top of the Rugby radio mast from a point 175m from the base, and found it 55°. If the measurements are correct to the nearest metre and nearest degree, find to 3SF the difference between the greatest and least possible values of the height of the mast.

   (b) Do the same calculation for Brian who was 20m away and measured the angle as 85°.

5   The fastest visible solid object ever recorded was a plastic disc projected at the Naval Research Laboratory in Washington, USA, in August 1980. It went fast enough to cross a room 4.29m wide in 28.6 microseconds, (28.6 millionths of a second.) Calculate, to 5SF, upper and lower bounds for its speed in km/s, assuming that the measurements are correct to 3SF.

6   The highest speed so far achieved by a standard production car is 217.1 mph. reached by a Jaguar XJ220 in June 1992.

   (a) At this speed, how many seconds does it take to go 1 mile?

   (b) If a car travels over a test mile in 16.2 seconds, and the mile is accurate to within 1% either way, and the time correct to 1DP, find upper and lower limits for the car's speed, in mph to 1DP.

7   If angle A is measured as 72° to the nearest degree, verify that the least possible values of the sine, cosine and tangent of A are 0.9483, 0.3007 and 2.9887 respectively, to 4DP. What is the least value of $\dfrac{1}{\tan A}$?

8   A ship in distress is reported to be 15km north and 10km east of a coastguard station. If these distances are correct to the nearest km, find, to 3SF, the least and greatest values of

   (a) the distance,

   (b) the bearing, of the ship from the station.

The effect of errors on calculations *(continued)*

9 A helicopter has landed 28km from its base, on a bearing of 074°, the distance and bearing both being correct to 2SF.

  (a) Sketch the shape of the region within which the helicopter must be, and calculate the area of this region in hectares to 3SF (1 ha = 10 000m^2.)

  (b) If the helicopter has co-ordinates x and y east and north of its base, calculate the least and greatest values of x and y, to 1DP.

10 If the data given in no.9 were known to be correct to 3SF instead of 2SF, can you predict how this would affect the size of the area you found in 9(a)? Check your prediction.

11 A tin of tomatoes has height 10cm and radius 3.5cm.

  (a) Express its volume as a multiple of π.

  Leaving π as a letter, find the percentage increase in the volume

  (b) if the height is increased by 5%,

  (c) if the radius is increased by 2%,

  (d) if both changes in (b) and (c) are made. Give answers exactly.

12 Investigate the percentage change in the area of a rectangle when the sides are increased by specified percentages p% and q%. Can you give an exact formula for the area's percentage change in terms of p and q? What simpler approximate formula applies when the changes are small?

Transforming graphs with Omnigraph

Log on and go into Omnigraph.

1   (a) Draw $y = x^2$, using <Alt> 2 to type the index ^{2}; then draw $y = x^2 + 1$ and $y = x^2 - 4$. Sketch the three graphs in your book, and say what transformation is needed to transform $y = x^2$ into each of the other two graphs. Check your answers by using the mouse to select the equation $y = x^2$, then typing <Alt> T for **Transformation**, (or click on this in the menu bar) then T for **Translation**, then give values for a and b in the vector that describes the translation.

   (b) If the graph of $y = f(x)$ is translated up b units, what is the new equation?

2   (a) How do you think $y = (x + 3)^2$ would be related to $y = x^2$? Check by drawing the new graph. Repeat with $y = (x - 4)^2$. Add these to your sketch, and write down the transformations needed to obtain them from $y = x^2$. Test your transformations.

   (b) If the graph of $y = f(x)$ is translated a units to the right, what is the new equation?

3   (a) Clear the screen using <Ctrl> <Delete> repeatedly, redraw $y = x^2$, then apply a translation $-4\mathbf{i} - 3\mathbf{j}$, i.e. $\begin{pmatrix} -4 \\ -3 \end{pmatrix}$, or 4 units left, 3 units down. Sketch the result, write down the equation of the new graph and check by using the computer to draw the graph.

   Repeat with translations

   (b) $3\mathbf{i} + \mathbf{j}$ (d) one of your choice.

   (c) $2\mathbf{i} - \mathbf{j}$ (e) If the graph of $y = f(x)$ is translated by $a\mathbf{i} + b\mathbf{j}$ what is the new equation?

4   If you are given the graph of $y = x^2$, how should you translate it to produce graphs of

   (a) $y = (x + 3)^2 + 2$ (c) $y = (x + 1)^2 - 4$?

   (b) $y = (x - 4)^2 - 3$ Check your answers.

5   (a) Clear the screen, choose **Custom** from the menu bar, then **Custom,** then click on **degrees** as the unit for angles. Type $y = \sin x$, then choose **Zoom** from the menu bar, click on **Rescale** and set the x scale from -500 to 500, the y scale from -4 to 4. Choose **Transformation**, then **Stretch**. Give the equation of the *stretch invariant line* (the line that won't move) as $y = 0$. This is the x-axis, so that the stretch will be in the y direction. Then set the *scale factor* to 3. Sketch the two graphs. What is the equation of the transformed graph? Write it down, and check by typing it in.

   Repeat with scale factors

   (b) 0.8   (c) -2.

   (d) If the graph of $y = f(x)$ is stretched in the y direction with factor k, what is the equation of the stretched graph?

6   Repeat no.5, but do the stretches with the stretch invariant line being $x = 0$, so that the stretches are in the horizontal direction. Use stretch factors

   (a) $\frac{1}{3}$

   (b) 2, and in each case write down the equation of the new graph and check by typing it.

   (c) Experiment with other factors. If the factor is k, what is the new equation?

7   (a) Clear the screen, type $y = \sin x$, then apply *successively* a stretch with factor $\frac{1}{2}$ in the x direction and a stretch with factor 1.5 in the y direction. (To do this, apply the first stretch, then highlight with the mouse the words **stretch line** $x = 0$ **factor** $\frac{1}{2}$ at the bottom left of the screen before doing the second stretch.) Write the new equation and check.

Transforming graphs with Omnigraph *(continued)*

(b) Highlight the first equation $y = \sin x$ again and apply an **enlargement** with centre $(0, 0)$, scale factor 3. Write and check the new equation.

What is the new equation if the graph of $y = f(x)$ is given

(c) stretches with factors m and n in the x and y directions,

(d) an enlargement with centre $(0, 0)$ and factor k?

8 What transformations applied to $y = \sin x$ will give the graphs of

(a) $y = 2\sin 2x$ (d) $y = \frac{1}{2}\sin(x + 100) - 2$?

(b) $y = 4\sin(0.8x)$ Check your answers.

(c) $y = \sin(x - 50)$

9 Start a new sheet and draw $y = f(x)$ with $f(x) = 2x^3 - x^4$; sketch this. How would the graph of $y = -f(x)$ be obtained from the first graph? What about $y = f(-x)$? $y = -f(-x)$? Try to sketch these graphs before drawing them on the screen, then check answers. Note that $f(-x)$ means $2(-x)^3 - (-x)^4$.

10 Repeat no.9 with $f(x) = x^2/4 + 2/x$. State what transformation is needed to transform $y = f(x)$ into

(a) $y = -f(x)$ (b) $y = f(-x)$ (c) $y = -f(-x)$.

11 Which of the transformations found in no.10 would leave unchanged the graph of

(a) $\sin x$ (b) $\cos x$?

What can you deduce about

(c) $\sin(-x)$ (d) $\cos(-x)$?

12 Clear the screen and type $y = \sin x$ and then $y = \sin x \cos x$. (Make sure that angles are measured in degrees, using **Custom**.) Set ranges for x and y as in no.5. What transformation is needed to go from the first graph to the second? Hence express $\sin x \cos x$ in the form $a\sin bx$, where a and b are constants to be found. Check your answer.

13 Clear the screen and type $y = \cos x$, then $y = \cos^2 x$. (This means $(\cos x)^2$, but can be typed in the usual abbreviated form.) How can the first graph be transformed to the second? Hence express $\cos^2 x$ as $p\cos qx + r$, with numerical values for p, q and r. Repeat with $\sin^2 x$, again relating it to $\cos x$. What can you deduce about $\cos^2 x + \sin^2 x$? Check your answers.

14 (a) Draw $y = x^2$ and $y = x^2 - 4x + 3$. How can the first graph be transformed to the second? Hence express $x^2 - 4x + 3$ in the form $(x + a)^2 + b$; check by multiplying out.

Repeat (a) with the second graph being $y =$

(b) $x^2 + 4x + 4$ (c) $x^2 + 8x + 12$ (d) $x^2 - 6x + 10$.

15 (a) By considering the expansion of $(x + a)^2$, try to express $f(x) = x^2 + 2x + 3$ in the form $(x + a)^2 + b$, and hence state the co-ordinates of the lowest point on the graph of $y = f(x)$. Check by drawing the graph, and repeat with $f(x)$ given by

(b) $x^2 - 10x + 21$ (c) $x^2 + 12x + 34$ (d) $x^2 - 5x + 5$.

16 Modify the method of no.15 to enable you to predict the lowest or highest point on the graph of each of the following. Sketch each graph and check using the computer.

$y =$

(a) $2x^2 - 12x + 18$ (c) $1 + 2x - x^2$

(b) $2x^2 + 8x + 5$ (d) $-40 - 24x - 3x^2$.

Solving cubics

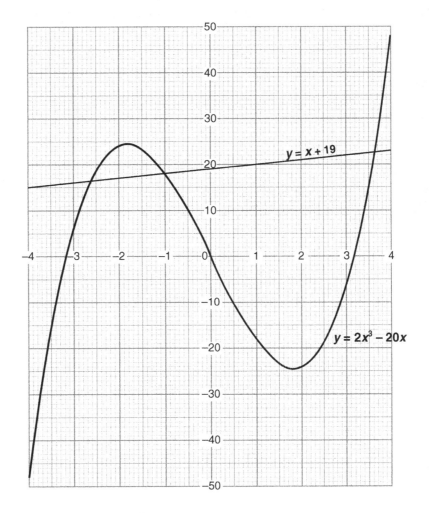

$y = x + 19$

$y = 2x^3 - 20x$

1   The figure shows graphs of $y = 2x^3 - 20x$ and $y = x + 19$.

   (a) What equation is satisfied by the values of x where the graphs meet? Find these values, and check by solving algebraically.

   (b) For which negative x is $2x^3 - 20x - (x + 19)$ greatest?

   (c) Find the range of positive values of x for which $2x^3 - 21x + 21 < 0$.

Now answer the following by drawing further straight line graphs on the sheet and, where indicated with *, by algebra (to 3DP where necessary).

2   Find for which values of x the value of $13 - 5x - (2x^3 - 20x)$ is

   (a)* 0   (b) positive   (c)* greater than 4.

3   (a)* Solve $2x^3 - 25x = 0$.   (b) Find the greatest value of $25x - 2x^3$ when x is positive.

4*   Solve $2x^3 - 17x + 3 = 0$.

5*   Solve $\dfrac{x^2 - 7}{2x + 1} = \dfrac{4}{x}$.

6*   Prove that $x^3 - 11x + 20 = 0$ has just one solution, and find it.

7*   How many solutions has $x^3 - 12x + 16 = 0$? Find them.

A1 Thinking decimals

The point of this sheet is for pupils to get answers by thinking about number relationships, and how the answer to a sum is changed when parts of the sum are changed in specified ways. Some of the questions invite finding approximate answers by making the input numbers simpler. None of the questions requires lengthy calculation, nor is a calculator needed.

1 $a = 1000$, $b = 0.001$, $c = 1000$, $d = 0.01$, $e = 0.001$, $f = 1000$, $g = 100$, $h = 0.01$, $i = 10\,000$, $j = 0.01$.

2 $a = 0.309$, $b = 51$, $c = 3.5$, $d = 100\,000$, $e = 10$, $f = 100$, $g = 0.172$, $h = 58$, $i = 16\,400$, $j = 0.0164$.

3 (a) 381.6   (b) 38.16   (c) 0.3816   (d) 381.6   (e) 381 600

4 (a) 40   (b) 0.4   (c) 0.04   (d) 0.04   (e) 400   (f) 40

5 (a) 25 300   (b) 2.53   (c) 2.53   (d) 0.0253   (e) 253   (f) 25 300

6 (a) 0.182   (b) 1820   (c) 18.2   (d) 1.82   (e) 0.182   (f) 1.82

7 (a) 1460   (b) 146 000   (c) 0.146   (d) 0.00147   (e) 1.47   (f) 147

8 (a) 10   (b) 0.1   (c) 100   (d) 0.01   (e) 10 000   (f) 0.0001   (g) N   (h) 0.001   (i) 1000

9 (a) 10   (b) 10   (c) 100   (d) 10 000   (e) 0.0001   (f) 10   (g) 0.01   (h) N   (i) 1   (j) 0.000 001

10 (a) 80   (b) 0.003   (c) 800   (d) 15   (e) 20   (f) 8   (g) 200   (h) 0.003   (i) 20   (j) 1.5

11 (a) 0.02   (b) 0.3   (c) 150   (d) 0.3   (e) 1.5   (f) 0.15   (g) 20   (h) 200   (i) 8   (j) 300

A2 Patterns and problem solving with algebra

Algebra is often experienced as a formal game without relevance to arithmetic. This sheet is meant to show how algebra can help explain number patterns and solve problems. It needs mainly only early algebra, plus a few instances of expanding brackets. The last part of the last question needs factorization. The sheet *Number patterns and algebra* uses more factorization.

1 (a) $n + 1$, $n + 2$. The total $3n + 3$ is always a multiple of 3; it is $3 \times (n + 1)$.

   (b) $n + 1$, $n + 2$, $n + 3$. The total is $4n + 6 = 2(2n + 3)$. This is twice an odd number, so is even but not a multiple of 4. (Or, the $4n$ is a multiple of 4, but the 6, though even, is not a multiple of 4.)

   (c) 1st × 4th $= n(n + 3) = n^2 + 3n$. 2nd × 3rd $= (n + 1)(n + 2) = n^2 + 3n + 2$. The difference is 2.

2 (a) $2n + (2n + 2) + (2n + 4) + (2n + 6) = 8n + 12 = 4(2n + 3)$, 4 times an odd number.

   (b) $(2n + 1) + (2n + 3) + (2n + 5) = (2n + 7) = 8n + 16 = 8(n + 2)$.

   (c) $(2n + 1)((2n + 7) = 4n^2 + 16n + 7$, while $(2n + 3)(2n + 5) = 4n^2 + 16n + 15$; the difference is 8.

3 (a) 29 and 31, 41 and 43, 59 and 61, 71 and 73. Totals are 60, 84, 120, 144; yes, all multiples of 12.

   (b) The primes are odd, so the middle number is even. They are not multiples of 3 (except in the case of 3 and 5) so the middle one is a multiple of 3, since every set of 3 consecutive integers has one multiple of 3. The twins are $6n - 1$, $6n + 1$, with total $12n$, clearly a multiple of 12. the exception with 3 and 5 occurs because 3 is itself prime and yet is a multiple of 3.

4 (a) Digit sums are 11, 13, 5, 17. Differences are 27, 63, 18, 72, all in the 9 times table.

   (b) $D = 9a$, a multiple of 9.

   (c) $N = 100a + 10b + c$, $S = a + b + c$, $D = 99a + 9b = 9(11a + b)$.
With 6 digits $D = 99999a + 9999b + 999c + 99d + 9e$, again a multiple of 9.

   (d) The difference between N and S is divisible by 9, so N and S leave the same remainder when divided by 9. If this is 0, both are multiples of 9; if it is 3 or 6, both are multiples of 3.

   (e) 1 (Digit sum is 28, this has digit sum 10, which has digit sum 1.)

5 (a) $10a + b = a + b + ab$, so $9a = ab$, and as a is not 0 for a two digit number, $b = 9$; the numbers are 19, 29, 39, 49, 59, 69, 79, 89 and 99.

   (b) $9a = 3ab$ so $b = 3$, giving 13, 23, 33...93. $N - S = 2P$ makes $9a = 2ab$, so $9 = 2b$, which is impossible as b is a digit and must be whole.

6 (a) $10a + b = 4(a + b)$ gives $6a = 3b$ so that $b = 2a$. The numbers are 12, 24, 36 and 48.

(b) 18   (c) 45   (d) 21, 42, 63 and 84.

7 (a) If $N = 10a + b$, then $R = 10b + a$. If R is 75% greater, it is 175% of N, i.e. $R = 1.75N$ as stated. We then get $10b + a = 17.5a + 1.75b$. Multiplying by 4 and rearranging, $33b = 66a$, so $b = 2a$; the numbers are 12, 24, 36 and 48.

(b) 45   (c) 72   (d) 15

8 No, the difference is always a multiple of 9. With 5 digits,
$10000e + 1000d + 100c + 10b + a - (10000a + 1000b + 100c + 10d + e) = 9999e + 990d - 990b - 9999a$.

9 Algernon was born in $1995 - a$, so $1995 - a = 56a$, giving $a = 1995 \div 57 = 35$.
Bertrand was 78, Cyril was 40, in 2000.

10 (a) 9   (b) $a + c - b$

11 $p + qr = (p + q)(p + r) = p^2 + pr + qp + qr$ gives $0 = p(p + q + r - 1)$, which is true if and only if either $p = 0$ or $p + q + r = 1$.

12 20 miles. (Uphill parts on the outward journey are downhill on the return, and vice versa.)

13 7.10 am

14 8100 crowns, 9 sons

15 Total in A was $3a$, then became $3a - 125$. $a = 135$. Similarly $b = 105$.

16 At 4.24

17 (a) 4, 12, 2, 32

(b) 6, 18, 2, 72 with operating number 6

(c) Let the total be T, the parts a, b, c, d, the operating number n and the result r. Then
$a + n = b - n = cn = d \div n = r$ gives $a = r - n$, $b = r + n$, $c = \dfrac{r}{n}$, $d = rn$, so that $r - n + r + n + \dfrac{r}{n} + rn = T$

or $\dfrac{r(2n + 1 + n^2)}{n} = T$, which can be rewritten as $\dfrac{r(n + 1)^2}{n} = T$.

This means that T must have a factor that is a square greater than 1, namely $(n + 1)^2$. Otherwise the division into parts cannot be done. If there is a square factor, identify one (there may be several), use it to find n, then $r = \dfrac{Tn}{(n + 1)^2}$, from which you can find the parts.

A3 Equations

The equations here all involve just multiplication and division, as do many equations in scientific applications. Solving them will give further practice in cancelling, and is best done without a calculator, though doing them with a calculator will still practice the algebraic skills required.

1	$\frac{2}{3}$	**11**	50	**21**	$2\frac{2}{3}$	**31**	0.22
2	$2\frac{1}{2}$	**12**	0.0167	**22**	$\frac{4}{5}$	**32**	$6\frac{2}{9}$
3	$1\frac{1}{6}$	**13**	0.075	**23**	0.036	**33**	0.05
4	1.6	**14**	63.7	**24**	0.9	**34**	6
5	12.6	**15**	0.02	**25**	24	**35**	6.48
6	4	**16**	35	**26**	0.12	**36**	9.8
7	40	**17**	32	**27**	0.9	**37**	0.0002
8	5	**18**	0.144	**28**	0.011	**38**	25.3
9	80	**19**	0.0084	**29**	0.0008	**39**	600
10	21	**20**	$\frac{11}{16}$	**30**	160	**40**	3×10^{-7}

41	$\frac{1}{4}$	46	15	51	$1\frac{1}{20}$	56	2000
42	20	47	0.0417	52	$\frac{1}{40}$	57	0.0168
43	3.5	48	5	53	160	58	42
44	$3\frac{1}{2}$	49	0.075	54	6	59	0.0002
45	$\frac{1}{6}$	50	12 500	55	0.00016	60	13.3 (or, exactly, $13\frac{1}{3}$)

A4 Cancelling

This encourages the development of fluency with numbers, and the use of factorisation, not as a formal algebraic operation, but as a means of simplifying arithmetic calculations. The questions should be done without a calculator, otherwise the benefit is largely lost.

1	$\frac{4}{5}$	16	80	31	6.2	46	11 572
2	$1\frac{5}{6}$	17	0.267	32	7.4	47	0.01
3	6	18	0.04	33	18	48	0.025
4	5	19	0.625	34	21	49	0.2
5	2.5	20	1.125	35	4.4	50	16
6	0.2	21	16	36	1	51	0.0467
7	1.67	22	24	37	$\frac{1}{2}$	52	3.08
8	0.1	23	21	38	$\frac{1}{6}$	53	3.17
9	5.6	24	0.165	39	100	54	11
10	2.5	25	17.6	40	10	55	0.099
11	1.2	26	0.07	41	0.000333	56	0.4
12	0.007	27	8.4	42	20	57	1.8
13	5	28	1.44	43	25	58	10
14	5	29	44	44	0.352	59	0.07
15	125	30	8	45	537.6	60	1.278

A5 Indices and standard form

Working fluently with powers, especially powers of 10, is an integral part of many scientific calculations. This sheet includes calculations involving actual physical constants.

1   (1) 10^4 (2) 10^8 (3) 10^{-1} (4) 10^3 (5) 10^{-4}
    (6) 10^3 (7) 10^{-14} (8) 10^3 (9) 3   (10) 10^{12}

2   (1) 10^{-2} (2) 10^{-10} (3) 10^5 (4) 10^{-3} (5) 10^5
    (6) 10^{-3} (7) 10^{10} (8) 10^{-3} (9) 3   (10) 10^{-12}

3   (1) 2×10^{15} (2) 10^{34} (3) 10^{47} (4) 8.1×10^{-14} (5) 4×10^{-10}
    (6) 9.6×10^4 (7) 2.7×10^{25} (8) 9×10^3 (9) 2.4×10^{-26} (10) 9.1×10^{-31}

4   (a) 1.5×10^8 km, 3×10^5 km/s   (b) 8min 20s   (c) 153 years

5   (a) 9.47×10^{12} km, 5.88×10^{12} miles   (b) 12.75km/s, $28500 = 2.85 \times 10^4$ mph

6   (a) $1836 = 1.836 \times 10^3$ (b) 5.977×10^{26}

7 2.5×10^{-8} mm

8 (a) $\frac{1}{3}$ (b) 0.01   (c) 64   (d) 0.0001

9 (a) 1.06   (c) 7.177%

     (b) £1000 × 1.06^n; after 10 years £1790.85   (d) 8.447%

     (For (c), if the rate is r%, the annual multiplier is $1 + \frac{r}{100}$, so we want $(1 + \frac{r}{100})^{10} = 2$.

     Now take the 10th root of each side, i.e. raise each side to the power $\frac{1}{10}$ to find $1 + \frac{r}{100}$ and then r.)

A6 Reading and drawing graphs

In nos. 1–3 the answers are as read from the graphs, correct to half a small square, and will not always agree with answers obtained by calculations. Answers to 4–6 have been calculated.

1 (a) 6s   (d) (1) After 1 and 5s   (2) at 0.3 and 5.7s

     (b) 45m, after 3s   (e) for 2.8s (from 1.6 to 4.4)

     (c) (1) 40m   (2) 30.5m   (3) 19.5m

2 (a) (1) 87.5m/s   (2) 40m/s   (c) 6 × 50 = 300m

     (b) (1) 1.2s   (2) 4.8s

3 (a) (1) $V = 55$, $A = 70$ (2) 215, 180   (c) (1) 375   (2) 450 km²

     (b) (1) 5.3   (2) 5.65   (d) $r = 3$ (or 0); volume and area both 216.

4 (a) Braking distance $b = v^2/20$ ft at $v$mph. (One way: tabulate values of b/v against v.)

v speed	0	10	20	30	40	50	60	70	80
a think dist	0	10	20	30	40	50	60	70	80
b brake dist	0	5	20	45	80	125	180	245	320
d total dist	0	15	40	75	120	175	240	315	400

     (b) Title etc

     (c) (1) 96.25ft   (2) 187.2ft

     (d) (1) Over 20mph   (2) Under 68.1mph   (3) 44.7mph

     (e) $\frac{15}{22} = 0.68$ s (the time it takes to go 1ft at 1mph, namely at 1760 × 3ft per 3600s.)

5 (a)

t	2	2.5	3	3.5	4	4.5	5	5.5	6	6.5	7	7.5	8
t^2	4	6.25	9	12.25	16	20.25	25	30.25	36	42.25	49	56.25	64
$5t^2$	20	31.25	45	61.25	80	101.25	125	151.25	180	211.25	245	281.25	320

     (b) Values of $10t - 5t^2$ are 0, 3.75, 5, 3.75, 0, finishing at $t = 2$.

     (c) Values of $20t - 5t^2$ are 0, 8.75, 15, 18.75, 20, 18.75, 15, 8.75, 0, finishing at $t = 4$.

         Values of $30t - 5t^2$ are 0, 13.75, 25, 33.75, 40, 43.75, 45, 43.75, 40, 33.75, 25, 13.75, 0, finishing at $t = 6$.

         Values of $40t - 5t^2$ are 0, 18.75, 35, 48.75, 60, 68.75, 75, 78.75, 80, 78.75, 75, 68.75, 60, 48.75, 35, 18.75, 0, finishing at $t = 8$.

     (d) Graphs

     (e)

v	10	20	30	40
T	2	4	6	8
H	5	20	45	80

         $T = \frac{v}{5}$, $H = \frac{v^2}{20}$. (1) 7s, 61.25m (2) 70m/s

6 (c) 7.6, 52.4 or 52.4, 7.6   (d) 66.5m by 13.5m   (e) 400   (f) 40cm

A7 Straight line graphs applied

1 (a)

x	0	2	4	6
y_A	0	50	100	150
y_B	20	60	100	140

   (b) graphs (c) 62.5, 70 min (d) $5\frac{1}{2}$ lb (e) from 3 to 5lb (f) y_A

2 (a) In each gear engine speed is proportional to car speed. Five lines are needed; there are 5 gears.

   (b) Gradients 200, 120, 80, 55, 45; $y = 200x$, $y = 120x$ etc.

   (c) 1350, 1650, 2400, 3600, 6000 rpm

   (d) 3150rpm

   (e) 1st: 5–20, 2nd: 8.3–33.3, 3rd: 12.5–50, 4th: 18.2–72.7, 5th: 22.2–88.9 mph

   (f) 2nd: $\frac{3n}{5}$, 3rd: $\frac{2n}{5}$, 4th: $\frac{11n}{40}$, 5th: $\frac{9n}{40}$. $n = 12\ 000$.

   (At 1mph in 1st the engine does 200rpm, and it takes 60min to go a mile at that speed.)

3 (a) 1.8; $F = 1.8C + 32$

   (b) −58, 176 and 374°F

   (c) −18, 21, 218°C (nearest integer)

   (d) −40

4 (a) F_1 at 10, F_2 at 160°C

   (b) F_1: $-40 < C < 60$, F_2: $110 < C < 210$

   (c) $5 < C < 15$

   (d) F_1 for weather, F_2 for oven temperatures

   (e) $145.3 < C < 177.6$ (to 1DP.)

A8 Number patterns and algebra

This sheet reinforces the fact that algebra is not just a formal game with letters, but is about numbers, and about patterns that work for all numbers; the use of letters allows these patterns to be seen to be true in general. The solutions and proofs depend very much on expanding and factorizing.

1 (a) $15 = 7 + 8$

   (b) the difference between the squares of any two consecutive integers equals the sum of the integers. Proof by expanding $(n + 1)^2$ to $n^2 + 2n + 1$; the difference $2n + 1 = n + n + 1$.

2 (a) $2\frac{1}{4}$, $6\frac{1}{4}$, $12\frac{1}{4}$, $20\frac{1}{4}$, $30\frac{1}{4}$ (c) $420\frac{1}{4}$ (e) 4225

   (b) It's integer × next integer $+ \frac{1}{4}$; expand $(n + \frac{1}{2})^2$.   (d) 10100.25

3 (a) $64\frac{2}{3}$; it is $\frac{2}{3}$ more than 8^2.

   (b) Quick way: middle number squared plus two thirds

   (c) $n^2 + \frac{2}{3}$

   (d) (i) $10000\frac{2}{3}$ (ii) 750 002

   (e) Middle number squared + 2; for k consecutive numbers the variance is $\frac{k^2 - 1}{12}$.

4 6, 24, 60, 120, 210. HCF is 6, true for all n because $n^3 - n = n(n - 1)(n + 1)$, a product of three consecutive integers, in which at least one is even, and one is a multiple of 3.

5 Remainders are all 1. True for all odd squares; either expand $(2n + 1)^2$ or, if k is odd, then $k^2 - 1 = (k - 1)(k + 1)$, a product of consecutive even numbers; one must be a multiple of 4.

6 (a) Yes, $8^2 - 7^2$ for example   (b) No: see below   (c) Yes, $8^2 - 2^2$ for example.

   For a difference of k we want $(x + y)(x - y) = k$. Let $k = ab$, with $a \geq b$. (The factors could be k and 1 if k has no other factors.) Taking $x + y = a$ and $x - y = b$ leads to $x = \frac{a + b}{2}$, $y = \frac{a - b}{2}$.

   But these are only integers if a and b have the same parity: both odd or both even. If k is odd, a and b will be both odd. If k is even, then since the factors can't both be odd they have to be both even; this is possible if and only if k is a multiple of 4. Thus, for k to be a difference of two squares, k must be either odd or a multiple of 4. (Hence the answer to (b) was No.) This question is usually found hard.

7 (a) 19. The answer seems to be the product of the first and last numbers, plus 1.

(b) $n(n + 3) + 1$. Proof is by expanding the square of this.

(c) 9701

8 (a) 31, 73, 421 (b) 111, 931 (c) It does. Check that $n^2 + (n + 1)^2 + (n(n + 1))^2 \equiv (n(n + 1) + 1)^2$.

A9 The effect of errors on calculations

1 Answers are given on the sheet.

2 (a) 31.185, 32.825 and 10.5, 32.5 (b) 31.918, 32.082 and 15.214, 16.868

3 (a) 4188.8cm³ (c) 1256.6, 1244.1, 1269.2 cm², 2.00%

(b) 4126.3, 4251.9 cm³, 3.00%

4 (a) 10.7m (b) 58.0m

5 150.44, 149.56 km/s

6 (a) 16.6s (b) 225.1, 219.3 mph

7 0.3153

8 (a) 17.3, 18.7 km (b) 031.5°, 035.9°

9 (a) It's part of a ring between two concentric circles, cut off between two radii. Area 48.9ha.

(b) x: 26.4 to 27.5, y: 7.3 to 8.1

10 It divides the area by 100.

11 (a) 122.5π cm³ (b) 5% (c) 4.04% (d) 9.242%

12 Exact change is $(p + q + \frac{pq}{100})\%$. For small changes this is approximately $(p + q)\%$

A10 Transforming graphs with Omnigraph

Software such as Omnigraph is an ideal tool for investigating how the equation of a graph changes when the graph is transformed geometrically. This sheet gives instructions which are specific to Omnigraph, but users of other software can equally do the questions here, provided that they know how to do things with the software.

The later questions explore trigonometric relationships, and introduce completing the square.

1 (a) Translations **j** and −4**j**, (up 1, down 4.) (b) $y = f(x) + b$.

2 (a) 3 to left, 4 to right (b) $y = f(x − a)$

3 (a) $y = (x + 4)^2 − 3$ (c) $y = (x − 2)^2 − 1$ (e) $y = f(x − a) + b$.

(b) $y = (x − 3)^2 + 1$ (d) own choice

4 Translate by

(a) −3**i** + 2**j** (b) 4**i** − 3**j** (c) −**i** − 4**j**

5 (a) $y = 3\sin x$ (b) $y = 0.8\sin x$ (c) $y = −2\sin x$ (d) $y = k\,f(x)$

6 (a) $y = \sin 3x$ (b) $y = \sin\frac{1}{2}x$ (c) $y = \sin(x/k)$

7 (a) $y = 1.5\sin 2x$ (b) $y = 3\sin(x/3)$ (c) $y = nf(x/m)$ (d) $y = kf(x/k)$

8 (a) Stretches, factor $\frac{1}{2}$ along x, 2 along y (c) Translation 50 to right

(b) Stretches, 1.25 along x, 4 along y (d) Stretch $\frac{1}{2}$ along y, translation −100**i** − 2**j**

9 Reflection in x axis; reflection in y axis; half turn about the origin.

10 (a) Reflection in x axis (b) reflection in y axis (c) half turn about origin

11 (a) half turn about origin (b) reflection in y axis (c) it = $−\sin x$ (d) it = $\cos x$

12 Enlargement with centre (0, 0), factor $\frac{1}{2}$. $\sin x \cos x = \frac{1}{2}\sin 2x$.

13 Enlargement with centre (0, 0), factor $\frac{1}{2}$ followed by translation by $\frac{1}{2}$**j**; $\cos^2 x = \frac{1}{2}\cos 2x + \frac{1}{2}$.

Enlargement with centre (0, 0), factor $\frac{1}{2}$ followed by reflection in x axis, then translation by $\frac{1}{2}$**j**;

$\sin^2 x = \frac{1}{2} − \frac{1}{2}\cos 2x$. Deduce that $\cos^2 x + \sin^2 x = 1$ for all x.

14 (a) Translation $2\mathbf{i} - \mathbf{j}$; $(x - 2)^2 - 1$

   (b) Translation $-2\mathbf{i}$; $(x + 2)^2$

   (c) Translation $-4\mathbf{i} - 4\mathbf{j}$; $(x + 4)^2 - 4$

   (d) Translation $3\mathbf{i} + \mathbf{j}$; $(x - 3)^2 + 1$

15 (a) $(x + 1)^2 + 2$; $(-1, 2)$

   (b) $(x - 5)^2 - 4$; $(5, -4)$

   (c) $(x + 6)^2 - 2$; $(-6, -2)$

   (d) $(x - 2\frac{1}{2})^2 - 1\frac{1}{4}$; $(2\frac{1}{2}, -1\frac{1}{4})$

16 (a) $2(x - 3)^2$; $(3, 0)$ lowest

   (b) $2(x + 2)^2 - 3$; $(-2, -3)$ lowest

   (c) $2 - (x - 1)^2$; $(1, 2)$ highest

   (d) $8 - 3(x + 4)^2$; $(-4, 8)$ highest

A11 Solving cubics

This sheet practises the use of graphs to solve equations and inequalities, as well as the algebraic approach based on factorization.

1 (a) $2x^3 - 20x = x + 19$; by graph $-2.65, -1, 3.65$; by algebra $-2.622, -1, 3.622$.

   (b) -1.8 to -1.9

   (c) $1.15 < x < 2.55$

2 (a) $-1, -2.098, 3.098$ (b) $x < -2.098, -1 < x < 3.098$ (c) $x < -2.366, -0.634 < x < 3$

3 (a) $0, \pm3.536$ (b) 3.4 (when $x = 2.0$)

4 $-3, 0.177, 2.823$

5 $-0.268, -3.732, 4$

6 -4

7 two solutions, -4 and 2; 2 is repeated.